22 Blessings in Disguise

Mary Ashun PhD

22 Blessings in Disguise

ISBN   1440463174

EAN-13   9781440463174.

Copyright © 2008 by Mary Ashun

Published by www.createspace.com

Comments to author: drmaryashun@rogers.com

THANKS:

To my husband Joe for suggesting I 'blog' (so I'd stop complaining?) and thus giving birth to this, our fourth child.

To my family and friends for giving me such good material, each and every day!

To Regina Doddington: thank you for encouraging me to do this.

To Tom Fusilli - English teacher extraordinaire - who shares my love of 'free-flowing prose' and who was so willing to 'mark' this work as one of his grade ten assignments. Word up to Michael Bromilow for having the patience to navigate the mysteries of formatting!

To my students: after ten years of teaching, it feels like you keep getting cloned and coming back to haunt me!

May you find your blessing somewhere within these pages!

TABLE OF CONTENTS

Blessing 1: Let it snow, Let it snow
Jeremiah 29: 4-11

I am Canadian.

I'm confident of this fact, but as winter approaches, I wonder how Canadian I am. I love seeing snowfall but I don't want to shovel it. I love seeing it on trees in my front yard, showering them with a light sprinkling in early December and then burdening them with their weight by February. But I can't stop the sinking feeling in my stomach that comes right after Thanksgiving...that winter is upon me once again and I have to 'survive' it. But how?

Being born in sunny Ghana, my great excuse is that I never grew up with snow. But that's a sort of lie because I also lived in England for part of my childhood. Second excuse is that most 'wintry' things are expensive. Have you ever tried signing up for a ski lesson? All sorts of fees to be paid and it's not like I can just walk there in my regular wintry duds and expect that it's sufficient for the slopes!

Being surrounded by other snow fearing black people doesn't help. Everyone treats the cold and snow like a huge painful disease that one just has to bear but I want to discard that attitude...I want to do something that says I enjoy snow. Convincingly.

Heidi, my white friend who is married to a fellow Ghanaian, has had some sort of success in that regard. She has managed to turn him into a snow loving black person...a great feat. Two years ago, she decided it wasn't enough to 'convert' just one Ghanaian; she was going to do it to a whole bunch of us! So, on a typical winter morning in January of 2004, Heidi invited three other African Canadian families to join them on a snow tubing fun day. We had amazing fun, with the kids having way more fun (of course) but did we do it again? Of course not!

Reminds me of the exiles who had been carried away to Babylon from Jerusalem. Jeremiah felt strongly that he needed to remind them of God's provision for their lives, even though they were so far away from home. They needed to be reminded that God had allowed them to be taken to Babylon and they were basically to make the most of it...by marrying, having children, planting gardens...basically, God wanted them to LIVE.

The neat thing is, it came with a wonderful reason: "For I know the plans I have for you says the Lord, plans to prosper you and not to harm you; plans to give you hope and a future". And now, as constant as death & taxes, another Canadian winter is upon us. Last year, our excuse was that there wasn't enough snow...even Heidi agreed with us. But this year, if it snows heavily enough, we've got to get out.

After all, this is Canada.
And in Canada, snow is here to stay.
And so are we. Lets be blessed wherever we live...even if its minus 25 degrees Celsius and oh so cold!!!!!

Update: It has hardly snowed! Oh man...I was so looking forward to the white stuff (snicker, snicker...)

Count your blessings

1. Where do you live? _____

2. Have you ever wished you lived somewhere else because of something you couldn't control...like snow?

Yes   **No**   **[circle one]**

3. If you could change one thing about where you currently   live   what   would   it   be?
   _____

4. Instead of trying to change that one thing, can you list a few ways <u>you</u> could adapt?

   _____

   _____

   _____

   _____

   _____

5. Let 'us' know what you did to make your 'snow' – *wherever you are* – a blessing.

   _____

   _____

   _____

   _____

Blessing 2: To react or not? That is the question!

Proverbs 15: 1

So this morning is typical of most mornings...rush, rush, rush with one of the kids doing something to get me all worked up like losing a hat for the gazillionth time, or wanting to go to the washroom just as we're pulling out of the driveway...nuff said.

We drive to 8-year old Kwam's school and there's a huge moving truck with a plank sticking out of it, parked in the lane closest to the door of the school – the 'near' lane. I can't get through this lane so I park in the passing lane. Now bear in mind that this is not the road – this is the school driveway that has two lanes – one closer to the door, then there's a median, then another lane. This outer lane is the one I parked on, ran out and into the building, said goodbye to Kwam and then ran back out. It took all of two minutes, no more. And the monstrous truck was gone.

"Thanks a lot for parking there!" shouted a man from his SUV, now passing through the lane closest to the door. I stood transfixed for just a second, shook my head, and then quickly sat in my car and drove off.

Why did this man assume that I had intentionally parked in the passing lane?

Why did he think that because he'd found the 'near' lane empty when *he* got there, that I must have found it empty too, when I arrived a couple of minutes before he did?

All these thoughts were coursing through my mind and I was getting angrier by the minute, wondering why we make so many assumptions when our decisions may be made based on just a few minutes. What if he'd arrived a minute before me and found the same situation I did? Would he have attempted getting into the driveway or allowed his child to get off on the busy road, cross it and walk to the school? Did he see the obstacle that prevented me from parking in the 'near' lane? Why do I want to punch this guy and make him listen to the reasons why I did what I did? Why does it hurt so much that I don't have a chance to explain? Will I ever see him again? Should I run if I do?

In Proverbs 15:1, the writer admonishes us to use gentle answers to turn away wrath because harsh words stir up anger. I know that, so why is it so hard? It's hard because our natural instincts are to react...all the time...to save ourselves. It's the survival thing; human sees predator, predator looks ready to attack, human draws out spear, human hopes predator has the sense to back off...you get the picture!

But being God, he knows why he admonishes us this way. God knows that anger unleashes the dirtiest parts of our souls...
Gosh, I have to pray to stop feeling like I still want to punch the guy...

Be blessed today with self-control, as you fight the urge to pummel someone...

Count your blessings

1. Can you identify with this situation?
    Yes   **No**   **[Circle one]**

2. Recount **your** situation.

    _____

    _____

    _____

    _____

    _____

3. Do you feel empowered today to exercise self-control, whatever the situation might be?
    Yes   **No**   **Maybe**   **[Circle one]**

4. If you've already exercised self-control, remind yourself how you did it...this is very empowering!

    _____

    _____

    _____

Be continually blessed!

Blessing 3: Free Mary
Matthew 14: 22 - 33

Taking a shower used to be a most onerous task. Water falling over my head, down my face, the struggle for air, the gulp of water....as I write this, my heart is beating faster than if a tiger was chasing me.

My fear of water began in 1975, when I was just seven years old. I was on a short camping trip with family friends and recall playing at the edge of a stream...or river...definitely a body of water. With my back turned and facing the flow, I tried to collect pebbles, sorting them, analyzing them, savoring the texture and critically discarding those that didn't meet my very discerning 7 yr old eyes and touch.

Before I knew it, what felt like a big wave had tossed me backwards and I was falling down what seemed like a waterfall...falling, falling, screaming, and swallowing.

When I turned sixteen, my friends threw a party for me at a local hotel. Not many knew I didn't swim and I wasn't about to tell. As I playfully bobbed in the water, my friend Kwame watched me carefully from the side of the pool. He was the only one who knew. Unbeknownst to me, as people swim in a certain direction, a current flows. As they raced across the pool my bobs, which I thought were at the same spot, were pushing me further and further away from the shallow end...that place where my feet always touch ground...and deeper into uncharted territory. One bob was all it took for me to realize I couldn't feel the floor...and then I started sinking. The same rushing feeling came back, I was swallowing more water than my body could handle and this felt like the end.

Thank God for Kwame.

Since then, I have tried twice to learn how to swim. I've never gone beyond the third lesson because that's when I have to go to the deep end. And I don't do deep ends. Which is ironic since I'm always trying to get others to go to their 'deep ends'. You see, I'm a teacher - a science teacher at a private school in Ontario. A 38 year old black woman with a Ph.D in Biochemistry, several publications to her credit and several students who will attest to the fact that I have made a difference in their lives...encouraging, coaching, pushing and aspiring them to do things they used to think were too difficult.

Why am I so afraid to do this one thing that my own three children are so comfortable with? And what right do I have to tell teenagers to take a leap of faith and walk through the door of learning I open for them everyday when I have refused to even acknowledge that my door to swimming exists?

In Matthew 14: 22 - 33, we read about Jesus walking on water. The disciples are stupefied...how is he doing this? They want so badly to go to him but they can't ever imagine walking on water. And yet, he repeatedly tells them to 'not be afraid'. Peter – as usual – says to Jesus "Lord if it's you, tell me to come to you on the water". And Jesus did. And Peter walked...on water. Something he would never, in his wildest dreams, think he could do.

Will I ever learn to swim? And if I do, can it ever become a lifelong recreational sport or will I just do it and never go near a pool again? What kind of an instructor or teacher will make the goal so relevant and attainable that with my fledgling faith in myself, I will entrust my safety and well being into his or her hands long enough to feel safe...with no ground beneath my feet? What are the implications for me as a teacher? How can all these experiences of me trying over and over again to accomplish something I consistently fail at, help me to *help* children who are tired of trying again...after failing so much?

You see, I'd like to try again...

Feel blessed if you've been able to conquer a recent fear. And, if you're like me with a fear that sometimes feels conquerable and other times not, feel blessed that it's **possible** to overcome fear...

Count your blessings:

1. Can you identify with my situation?

Yes   **No**   **[Circle one]**

2. As you read this chapter, what particular fear came to mind?

_____

_____

3. Have you tried recently to overcome this particular fear?

Yes   **No**   **[Circle one]**

4. How many times?

Once   twice   thrice   I lost count!   [Circle one]

5. What steps do you think you can take to overcome this fear and turn it into a blessing?

    1. _____

    2. _____

    3. _____

When you're up to it, write a prayer from the heart...

Blessing 4: So they all rolled over and one fell out
1 Samuel: 25

There were two in the bed and the grumpy one said:
" Why can't I sleep in this bed without anyone kicking me?"

It's about 2 am and as usual, five-year-old Jojo has had another 'nightmare' (basically, he just wakes up to go and pee) and has to come to dad and mom's room (to say hi?).

When he comes to mom's side of the bed, she carries him back to his bed, tucks him in, waits a few minutes to make sure he's on his way to dreamland, and then tiptoes quietly back to her bed to try and catch her dream at just the place she left it. Contrast that with dad's methods of dealing with children-who-disturb-parents-at-night: huddles them in (sometimes I think he plays football in his sleep!), covers all three with the quilt and then tries his hardest to catch *his* dream. Any guesses whose side of the bed Jojo visits nine times out of ten?

So its déjà vu all over again but this night, my back has gone AWOL. A gnawing feeling at the back of my mind is saying I need to lose weight – maybe that's why my body is feeling like it belongs to someone else.

We go through the rigmarole once more and as usual, things are so tight in the bed (since Jojo the sleep stealer is in it with us!), that Joe leaves the bed, trudges downstairs, turns on his audio bible and proceeds to have a serene devotional which eventually lulls him back to sleep. Cut to me in bed with the
rampaging bull known in sleepy parent circles as Jojo. Even though Joe thinks he's done the thoughtful thing by putting a pillow in between us, my lower back is still suffering from the constant kicking. Thing is, tonight, I can barely move. On other nights, I'd either tell him to cut it out or I'd carry him back to his bed. Tonight, I can't even move myself away from the onslaught of long 5-year-old feet and a head that seems so much bigger at night. I'm crying silently and wondering why Joe thinks he's done me a favour...why didn't he just take the child back to bed?

I'm getting angry now. Wondering why Jojo's comfort is of far more consequence than mine. Am I being selfish? Am I a bad mother for wanting some space? Will I miss this when I'm sixty and Jojo is all grown up and lives away from home? Will I look back in nostalgia and say:

"Oh, I wish I'd let him pummel my body into a dithering mass...how I miss the pain". I THINK NOT!

Now how am I going to deal with Joe? When I finally wake up (actually, open my eyes since I really haven't been able to sleep), do I congratulate him, in a bitter voice, on his good night's rest and wait for him ask me how mine was? Do I immediately let him know how I feel about him abandoning me to Jojo's dark side? Do I plead with him in a sorrowful tone to not do this again?

I'm thinking of biblical Abigail at this moment...full of wisdom, knowing how to diffuse a bad situation, sensing where her priorities lay and definitely not doing or saying things when she was angry. The bible calls her 'discerning and beautiful"....mmmhhh...can I be both this morning?

When I think of how many people go to sleep on things other than beds, I am grateful I have a real bed. Even if I have to share it! I'm going to get up, have a great attitude and feel blessed today, knowing that we are so fortunate to have the creature comforts we have.

Update: Yay! I was discerning and beautiful (in spirit - since my morning get up wasn't really Essence magazine material!) I didn't sound angry at all, just stated matter of fact what we should do with the sleep-stealer. Together, we shall battle the little thing!

Count your blessings

1. Can you identify with my situation?

    Yes   No   Sort of   [Circle one]

2. Do you sometimes wonder if you are a good parent?

    Yes   No   Sort of   [Circle one]

3. Have you ever wished that you'd wake up one morning and your children would be all grown up? With no hang-ups?

    Yes   No   Sort of   [Circle one]

4. Are you scared they're growing up too fast?

    Yes   No   Sort of   [Circle one]

5. If you're not a parent (yet?), how do you think you will react when those little ones come along?

    _____

    _____

Pray that you will be blessed with Grace today!

Blessing 5: The Oreo Cookie Dilemma
Exodus 2:11 – 15

T he racial divide continues to grow. This afternoon, while standing behind a white lady waiting to be served coffee, I heard her telling the cashier how much darker she was getting, as she grew older. I listened, quietly musing about how concerned she was. The cashier (who could see me) sort of let the conversation tail off as I shifted from foot to foot so the lady in front of me turned and that's when I said:
"I know what you mean...I've been growing darker too".
Supposed to be a joke. But she looked so uncomfortable, I had to say I was joking...again. Sheesh!

Reminded me of the time I went to pick Kwam up from gymnastics but Joe had passed by and picked him up already. The poor lady at the front desk couldn't remember the name of the person who had picked him up, only that he wore a black leather jacket with a baseball cap.
"And what else?" I prompted gently.

"Umh...he wasn't very tall and he wasn't very short"
Oh, I thought. That helps. Most people are neither tall nor short! As I rolled my eyes, I noticed some discomfort creep into the lady's face...she wanted to say something but couldn't.

"Umhh...Kwam looked like him". Yah, that helps – especially when you think that people who aren't black think most black people look the same!

So, do I take her out of her misery? Do I dare utter that word that she is so afraid to use? Do I help her *not* to feel like she's being racist? And if I do, have I solved anything?

After mulling over what seemed like HER Waterloo, I very casually said: "Was he black?" The floodgates opened, the mountains tumbled, and the sea was split in two! She was free!

"Yes, yes" she said eagerly, wiping her forehead like she'd run a marathon. "I didn't know how to say it...didn't want to sound like...like...

"You saw him only as a colour?" I offered gladly.

"Well yah", she said.

Yah, I thought...

Don't we do these things everyday? Describe people based on lots of inconsequential things that are not definitive? Wearing a leather jacket. A baseball cap. And so on.

When really, just saying black, says a whole lot – especially if there are hardly many black people where you're looking... like a gymnastics camp for boys!

My wonderful friend Virginia told me a similar story that happened to her in Colorado. She and her husband were out for dinner to celebrate a milestone in their lives together. She got out of the car to 'check in' while her husband found a parking spot in the busy lot. The receptionist was very attentive, and chatted with her about this and that. She eventually led her to her table and Virginia waited patiently for her husband to show up. Her husband Gareth showed up at the front desk and mentioned to the receptionist that he was joining his wife. He politely waited for the receptionist to direct him to Virginia.

He waited while she checked her list.

And waited while she scanned the room.

Then she said, "I'm sorry sir but there's no one here waiting for you". To which Gareth replied, "Yes there is...she walked in here no more than 10 minutes ago.
The lady looked confused. Was this guy crazy?
Then she got a brilliant idea!

"Sir, what name is the reservation under?"
"Bridges" Gareth said.
After a very pregnant pause,
"Oh...but...umhh...please follow me sir. So sorry about the confusion".

You see, Gareth is white. And Virginia? Well, she's black.

I realize that I may be so comfortable in my blackness that I don't mind these things any more. Neither does Virginia. And yet some black people may mind and find it awfully offensive.

In today's reading from Exodus 2, Moses makes a dangerous decision based on race. He has recently discovered he's Hebrew, (the 'black' of his society) and not Egyptian (the white of his society). Trying to prove his *hebrewness*, he murders an Egyptian who is fighting a Hebrew. You know where that gets him?

In a desert! Away from his own people, in a land he didn't know, until the Lord knew he was ready to be a Hebrew without killing an Egyptian!

How comfortable are you being what God has made you? Lets feel blessed today, whatever colour we are, knowing that whatever God's plan for your life, you CAN accomplish a whole lot, whether black, white, yellow or red!

Count your blessings

1. Can you identify with my situation?

   Yes   No   Sort of   [Circle one]

2. You may have numerous examples but can you just summarize one?

   _____

   _____

   _____

   _____

3. Have you ever been ashamed to be whatever colour you are?

   Yes   No   [Circle one]

4. In what way have you felt your colour being a blessing?

   _____

   _____

   _____

   _____

Blessing 6: You're embarrassed?
Genesis 27: 1 – 38

"Bye mom!"

With this announcement, my buck-toothed, braces needing 8-year-old Kwam, bounded out of our '99 Taurus through the front doors of his school. As I got out of the car and struggled to keep up with him, I thought it ironic that on a day when I had called in sick, I'd be able to walk INTO the school with him for his Before School program at 7:30am. As I tried to keep up with him, he turned around and asked why I was following him.

"Why not" I said
"Well, umhh...that hat...it's...you know..."
"Yes?"
"It's sort of weird mom".

Sheesh, I thought. I knew my hair looked matted underneath and this green woolen hat was what I needed to make me look presentable enough to drop him off, rush back home and climb right back into bed with my Rooibos tea. But he was embarrassed. To be seen with a scruffy looking mom. Aw sheesh!

I smiled. Because, I remembered. That my grandma used to do the same thing. Bad behaviour was rewarded with "I'm going in to school with you tomorrow"

and that was enough to conjure up images of absolute embarrassment – grandma with
no teeth, hobbling after me in the hallway for all to see we shared several genetic traits. So I understood. And did what any normal mom would do.

"Well honey, just tell them I'm your new nanny from Wakothingi"
"M-o-m, there's no such thing as Wakothingi", he said.
But he smiled.
And I knew he understood too. A high school teacher in suburban Toronto, I've been embarrassed more than once...ok, several times, but the one that immediately comes to mind was a day that started off pretty normally, meaning I was yelling and screaming for Jojo and Kwam to get out of bed and into their school gear.

So, as usual, I drop Jojo off and then Kwam but today I forgot Kwam and just continued on Derry Road...to school! Well Kwam being Kwam (i.e. seemingly clueless about the world around him), he said nothing so I continued driving. Mercifully, I wasn't out of Mississauga before I realized that I hadn't dropped him off so I had to turn around and take him in. So, I was almost late for the special assembly at 8:40am and just managed to slip in without it being so obvious.

The assembly was great. A black guy called Anthony McLean was talking about bullying and the kids really responded. He ended by saying he was going to freestyle...and he asked if they knew what freestyle was! I think because he saw the sea of white faces, he thought they wouldn't know anything about rap but research shows that the market for rap is actually in the white community. So, he asked them to give him any topic and he'd rap to it so the topics started flowing – from Canada to dirt to Olympics to Soviet Russia! He rapped to all of them and he was really good. Then he said he was going to teach someone who couldn't rap how to rap and asked for volunteers.

I could hear everyone shouting for Jun Li – Korean guy who thinks he is really black and can dance, rap, freestyle (I think that's rap?) ...name it, he can be seriously black.

Then Anthony said no, he wanted a teacher...yah, you know where this is going...everyone screamed for me! Oh my, I was mortified...how was I going to rap for crying out loud? I was literally dragged up and had to rap! He said "1,2,3,4,5,6,7,8 and 4 and 8 should rhyme ok?" To which, I stupidly nodded. Then he said 'I'll start, you finish 1,2,3, cat' then turned the mike to me and I said "5,6,7, dog"...to which you could not find one dry eye or a bottom on a chair! Everyone was almost on the floor laughing so hard because apparently, I was supposed to say a word that rhymed with cat and I said dog!!! And I had noooooo clue!!!!!!!! Oh God, I was so glad I couldn't blush because I would have been burning! The rest of it went downhill from there and he noticed my embarrassment and allowed me to escape!

The interesting thing was how the student body perceived me afterwards. Several came up to me to congratulate me for being such a good sport...for pretending to NOT know how to rap...because as a black person, the consensus was, I must know how to rap! But, I argue to myself, I just heard of 50 cent – the rapper - last year!

Image is everything...especially when you are a kid. And working with teenagers....it definitely is the thing! However, when we let image dictate how we handle situations, it can quickly get out of hand. In Genesis 27, Jacob pretends he is Esau to get the blessings that Isaac meant for Esau. He put on an image that wasn't his, in order to get something that was not his. And look how that ended; enmity between brothers and their descendants even to this day. Sometimes when we are dissatisfied with our 'lot in life', it is even more tempting to become something we are not.

Lets pray for ourselves, that God gives us the strength to be proud of who we are, even when it may not be the 'in' thing to be!

What a blessing it is, to get embarrassed and grow from it!

Count your blessings

1. Can you identify with any of the scenarios described in 'You're Embarrassed'?

   Yes   **No**   **Sort of**   **[Circle one]**

2. What is your most embarrassing moment? (It doesn't leave this page – I promise!)

   _____

   _____

   _____

   _____

3. How have you moved on? (Short of moving to another planet?)

   _____

   _____

   _____

   _____

Be grateful that your embarrassing moment is probably not as bad as someone else's! What a blessing eh?

Blessing 7: Supersize me
Acts 5: 1- 11

No one ever told me I'd need 50 inch biceps to push a grocery cart around a store but that's what I'm currently thinking...as I try to wield a decidedly unwieldy cart through a maze of aisles packed full of things I can't possibly need, passing people who can't possibly eat all that's in their carts and trying hard not to knock over the 80 year old woman at the corner of each aisle enticing me to try a broccoli and chicken filled mini quesadilla!

So all this had me thinking...who invented this Saturday morning phenomenon? One that sees me going to the store to pick up six things and coming out with fifty things? One that has me wondering if the self-serve checkout is faster than the 'you serve me' cashier checkout. One that has me wondering if the name brand liquid soap costing $5.99 is really better than the no name brand that costs 'just $2.99'...

Enough already!

Of course I've heard about how much we consume and all, but has anyone ever stopped to wonder how it feels like to be hungry? Of course not! Many of us don't even know what I'm talking about. And what about the incredible feeling of achievement we feel when we buy something new? Even if we don't need it? I think there must be a gene for needless shopping – you have it or you don't and most men don't. Just as most genes in our bodies are 'turned on' and 'off' at certain periods, there must be something like that too – that makes us want to shop...or not. And sometimes, it's switched on...big time. And for some of us unfortunately, it's never switched off. It's defective...there's a mutation of the gene...so we need therapy!

I've never wanted much in the way of personal possessions. So long as it looked good, then I'd have it. I think the most expensive shoes I've ever bought for myself have been $65. For clothes, I've never spent more than $120 on any one thing with my preferred price range being anything less than $29.99...yah, I can be quite cheap...but classy cheap if there's such a thing.

So now, Joe and I are in the market for a new car and we seriously need one. Our Taurus is now eating us alive and we've
loved it for so long that we've tolerated all its shenanigans...the latest $2300 for some mechanical thing or other...I almost choked when the mechanic told me – in fact, I think I did.

We think we want a van – with three boys, we do need something that allows their individual body parts to remain separate from the next person's body parts! But I love the way an SUV looks...it's powerful looking, shaped nicely...and is snazzy! But there's hardly any space at the back and with all the bags and junk we normally transport in the course of our daily lives, is that a wise choice? Joe is prowling around auctions like a hungry grizzly bear...looking for leather seats in $15,000 rejects so we're each trying to get deals...in our own ways – me in newspapers, Joe, out on the road. Will this search for better ever be over?

Joe and I are constantly reminding ourselves that we don't want to be like Ananias and Sapphira. In Acts 5, we meet these typical westerners – rich, getting richer every day, and wondering how best to keep a lot while giving out as little as possible. Their church encourages them to share a portion of what the Lord has blessed them with, but greed starts to eat away at them, gnawing like a relentless rat, beckoning to their need for more. And before they realize it, they have decided to keep back a lot of their wealth instead of sharing it.

Looking for something better, especially when you can afford it is not wrong. Relentlessly looking to get things you can't afford and **not** looking for ways to enrich other lives with what the Lord has blessed you with **is** wrong.

How much have we given back? Let's bless others today in the same way the Lord has blessed us. Amen.

Update: We got the van with all the bells and whistles so now the children want to live in it...we think that's cool; we didn't think we'd be empty nesters so soon!

Count your blessings

1. How much do you **needlessly** spend on shopping each week?

   <$50 $50 - $100   Over $100   [Circle one]

2. Have you ever purchased something and returned it because you felt guilty for spending so much?

   Yes   No   I do it all the time...help!!!!!!!
   [Circle one]

3. Can you make a pledge that every time you feel the urge to spend, you will make a mental note of where it could be better spent? Write your pledge here.

   _____

   _____

   _____

What a blessing it is that we have something to give?

Blessing 8: The House at Pooh Corner
Luke 3: 1- 19

I walk into a world different from my own every day of the week. As a black teacher in a predominantly white school, I am always conscious of the differences in how I dress, how I talk, how I am perceived and ultimately judged. But that doesn't stop me from being me...which for me means asking questions about why things can't be done differently...to effect change.

One of those moments came three years ago in a grade 12 chemistry class of 8 students, all from very affluent homes. One student was recounting his experience in an unsafe part of Toronto, an encounter involving a drive by shooting. As his classmates listened to this incredulous tale from another side of their planet, he turned to me and said,
"You know what I'm talking about Dr. Ashun – you're black".
To which I replied very stiffly,
"Yes I'm black, but I've never observed a drive-by shooting".

What was I going to do to dispel some of the myths continuously perpetuated by irresponsible media? In my usual risk taking fashion, I organized a trip to Ghana, the place of my birth. Surprisingly, 6 students signed up for the trip to deepest darkest Africa and what a trip it was! We visited Slave Castles on the Gold Coast, watched a crocodile display the wonders of its majestic pointed teeth, walked on top of the rain forest and along the way, found out that not everyone in Africa had AIDS or a distended belly or spoke no English.

Thus was the Global Learning Initiative born. One that seeks to educate through experience and travel and one that continues to challenge. Last year, we went to Brazil. In January 2007 we went to the Dominican Republic and in March 2007, we will go to New Zealand. As I expose students to a world outside of their own, I look forward to them asking why I pick the countries I do. Ghana, because I was born there, and what I remembered of it was not what I heard people say about it in North America. And I needed to see it again, through their eyes.

Brazil, because the culture is so rich and the sights are memorable. And of course, we all want to find out if they clone all those soccer players! Dominican, because it's closer to home and our students need to feel needed...and there are several missions set up in the tiny Caribbean country. New Zealand...well, it can't be all about sheep, right? And I want students to know that there are aboriginals in places other than Northern Ontario!

We've all been blessed with amazing experiences and backgrounds but I wonder how often we 'evangelize' these experiences. In Luke 3, we meet John the Baptist, a guy who by today's standards would be described as seriously wacky and out of touch. Living in the desert, dressed in rags and eating locusts and honey...eeewwwwww! Talk about someone with background and experiences unlike those he preached to! He didn't let that stop him from letting them know that the Lord was coming. And the Lord was right around the corner.

We can all be evangelists – sharing our experiences and sharing the Lord's love. Can you think of a way that you can bring these experiences into your home, place of work, place of worship or where you hang out? The Lord is bound to speak
through you *to* someone...and there's no doubt you'll be changed too.

I know that there are programs similar to ours in several schools in Ontario but I doubt if many of them were started by a teacher who felt so different that she had to invite her students into her world. Like Winnie the Pooh, I'm always looking at simple ways of finding 'honey' and then sharing it with my unlikely group of friends. Inviting them into my 'house' is my way of bringing some understanding into the '100 Acre Wood"!

Count your blessings

1. What amazing experience have you had that you could share?

    _____
    _____
    _____
    _____
    _____
    _____

2. Did you know that there are many teachers looking for people to come and share their experiences with students? Make a note below to call your child's teacher, write to them or maybe pop into your neighborhood school and talk to the principal. You never know how you could be a blessing to a child...

Blessing 9: The 'war' ain't over
2 Samuel 18

Its morning and I can hardly see it through all the grog of being awake most of the night. My eyes feel heavy and my feet feel like I've had lead straps tied to them. I drifted in and out of mindless dreams – being awake and yet feeling asleep while switching the nebulizer on and off.

Jojo had an asthma attack last night. He was wheezing so badly, I actually got scared. This is saying something since I tend to err on the side of 'this isn't that bad...let's wait it out'. Whereas the kids just have to sneeze and Joe is at Emerge. And not just any emerge...at the Hospital for Sick Children Emerg! Around 11:30, it had gotten so bad that I gave in and called Gwen (my sister in-law who's a nurse) who came over promptly with her husband Joe and checked him out with her stethoscope and all. She said he was pretty bad and gave him a large dose of ventolin using the nebulizer, so we all sat and watched the thing work...till about 1:00am when she assured us that the worst was over. After she and Joe left, of course, Joseph and I couldn't get back to sleep. We were worried...as all parents tend to be when their little ones are sick.

Have you read 2 Samuel lately? What an amazing story of sadness, disappointment and love is played out in that chapter? David has many sons and Absalom is supposed to be the hottest (for those not into teen lingo, hot means very handsome!). He has leadership ability but is quite hotheaded and impatient (like many kids!). He decides he can do the king job better than his dad (no kidding!) and proceeds to recruit other losers in the kingdom to mount some sort of a rebellion. What a child!

Of course he doesn't succeed. In fact, he is killed in the uprising. And when David is told, he is incredibly heartbroken. His courtiers can't believe the king is mourning the child who plotted to overthrow his father. His army commander Joab reprimands him for belittling the efforts his army made to stave off Absalom's attack. Because of the army's dedication, David, his wives, concubines, other sons and daughters were all saved.

So why was David so sad?

I recall a Ghanaian proverb, which translated, literally means, "*In defeat, those who stayed home and didn't fight in the war think those who went, didn't fight at all*". I know it sounds a bit weird but translations do that...they take the meat right out of it! Reason why I thought about this proverb is...you never know the sacrifices and tough times you will face when you have kids until you have them. And yet many of us don't learn anywhere, the skills and understandings you will have to cultivate when children come along:

* The ease with which you willingly give up a lot...for them. Neat thing is, you actually don't miss those things too much, after you give them up for the ones you love.
* The frustrations that come when they don't see things your way...the right way...and try to go their own way.

* The joy of seeing them succeed at what they do...while praying that they don't get puffed up with pride.
* The relief when you hear someone say "That child is so well behaved, so well brought up" and you realize they're talking about your child.

David would have loved to experience all of these with Absalom instead of just the second one; those experiences that you can only have when 'you go to war". For those of us with children, lets let every annoyance seem like a blessing; an awesome opportunity to be used by God to shape a life. For those without biological children of their own, look around...there are many 'children' who would benefit from having you in their lives....

Be a blessing today!

Count your blessings

1. Have you recently been up at night, losing sleep because of a loved one?

   Yes   No   [Circle one]

2. Do you sometimes wish your loved ones would realize how much you care...and maybe say thanks...especially your teen?

   Yes   Doesn't matter to me
   Too tired to think!

3. Think of one child today...maybe yours but it doesn't have to be. What needs does this child have – material, spiritual, mental? How can you be a blessing to this one child?

   _____

   _____

   _____

   _____

   _____

Blessing 10: An apple a day
John 5: 1 - 9

The place smelled of sickness and disease and I wondered how anyone could go in there and come out not feeling ill. And as I made my way to one of the seats in the waiting area, it struck me as very many, the number of people who get sick everyday.

This was an afternoon like many others – Jojo exerts himself so hard that Jojo needs his puffer. Puffer is close to empty and is not very effective. Jojo needs intervention. Mary and Joe rush Jojo to the hospital. Emergency is a joke...who ever lied to us that this is the place you go to, when there is an emergency? There are all sorts of people here - sick...sad...helpless...and grumpy. Jojo is by far the healthiest looking person in this place. We wait. Nothing new there. The health system has become like that and everyone here is wondering...when is anyone going to come and see me?

Jojo, while restlessly showing his boredom, kicks an old lady who is there with her teenage granddaughter. All hell breaks lose and this old lady goes ballistic. On a five year old! I scooped him up before she could use any of her weapons of mass destruction and found a corner to cradle him while we waited for his 'emergency' to be serious enough to push him to the front of the queue. I felt dejected. And I wasn't even sick. Why do we get sick?

Why can't our bodies go on forever? Well sort of forever? And even when we eat all the good food and do

our regular body 'oil change', we can still end up with diseases that hasten our pilgrimage to a hospital - that place where we're supposed to feel better but for the most part don't.

Recall the man in the healing story found in John 5. He'd been patiently waiting to be healed for thirty-eight years. Imagine that! Our national health system is so clogged that some specialist appointments can take six months and that's way too tortuous to bear. This man must have felt like he'd never get healed because when the angel stirred the water, he had no help getting into the pool...what a despondent feeling? He must have thought more than once, about the possibility of never being sick. And we do too but more so when we're in a hospital.

Lord give us the grace to be thankful for our health and to pray for daily healing of our bodies...they can break down after all!

Count your blessings

1. When was the last time you had to go to the hospital?

_____

2. Did you experience what I did....that feeling of helplessness?

    Yes　　　**No**　　　　　　**[Circle one]**

3. What blessings can you recount that have to do with your health?

_____

_____

_____

_____

_____

Blessing 11: Equilibrium
Acts 4:13

Today, I started the Chemical Systems & Equilibrium unit with my grade 12's and tried to explain Le Chatelier's principle, which states that:

"When a system at equilibrium is placed under stress, the system will tend to shift in a direction that will annul the effect of that stress".

In English, this means that if I slap you, you'll probably want to slap me back because that will seem to alleviate the temporary stress that I placed on you! So, I'm trying to explain this to my students and all I'm getting is that blank stare that says, "What a load of ---- (not a bad word, be creative!). I was wondering how to explain the concept of equilibrium to these students and talk about what it meant for a system to react against a stress applied to it.

Ergo, have you heard of the duck swimming apparently smoothly on the lake? Well, this duck that looks like it's just having fun sailing along has its feet furiously paddling beneath the water...but you can't see that; all you see is a peaceful duck. When a system is at equilibrium, reactions are still going on beneath it all, but you can't see that. There are forward and reverse reactions that are constantly going on and when the rate of one equals the rate of the other, bingo – you are at equilibrium... that place when it all seems ok.

But, and this is a big but, things can come along that can momentarily disrupt this equilibrium – this peaceful state of affairs. To explain this, I picked the one area that most kids would understand – relationships.

"So", I continued in my know-it-all adult voice, "Giovanni is attracted to Danielle but Danielle doesn't reciprocate the feeling. The reaction of Giovanni liking Danielle is the forward reaction and it's going at an appreciable rate but the reverse reaction i.e. Danielle liking him – isn't happening at all. Looks sort of like this:

Giovanni →→→Danielle

Then he asks her out on a date, something casual, with a group of friends. She's ok with this and so she says yes. While on the date, she realizes he's not such a dweeb so she starts to like him. Now, the reaction from Danielle to Giovanni is going much better – not as fast as the one from him to her, but it's still happening.

Stay with me here, it gets better. Giovanni asks her for a second date and brings flowers. She's really into him now and is wondering if he will ask her out, officially...and he does and she says she'll think about it. In teen girl world, this usually means, "wait till I talk to my friends to find out what they think"! So she does and they're all like "he's so cool, go for it girl" and so she says yes! This is what the reaction now looks like:

Giovanni ⇔⇔⇔ Danielle.

Notice that the arrows go both ways. So, they are now at equilibrium. Everything seems perfect on the surface but like everyone who's ever fallen in love, you know that that's when the agony begins.
"Does he like me as much as I like him?"
"Will she ever stop calling me?"
"What outfit shall I wear that he hasn't seen me in?"
"I wonder if I can borrow dad's car for the movies?" And so on and so forth.

So pretty soon, as sure as death and taxes, a stress appears. Like chemical reactions that have stresses applied in the form of temperature & pressure changes, catalysts etc, relationships too have their stresses. Let's call this particular stress Allison.

Allison is pretty, petite and oh so available. Giovanni is seen talking to her and acting interested. This is a no-no for any high school relationship. Recall that Giovanni and Danielle, until this point, are at equilibrium. Danielle hears this – in high school, everyone hears everything – and the equilibrium is immediately disturbed. What does she do? She thinks she might wait to talk to him and find out what's going on. The feelings of mistrust, unease and anxiety are all byproducts of that stress. After talking to him and realizing it's not a big deal – Allison was just trying to recruit him to be a male model in her fashion show – Danielle and Giovanni are back at equilibrium.

That state when it seems nothing is wrong.

Chemical systems do the same thing. One very useful equilibrium is that present in the blood. When a stress is applied – in the form of a toxin- the equilibrium is disrupted but the system will shift either in the forward or reverse direction to get rid of the toxin and restore the body back to equilibrium.

Jesus had an amazing relationship with his disciples. He was there for them and for most of the time, they were there for him too. They ate together, shared together, traveled together and helped each other. This relationship was so strong that even after he was taken from them, stresses that were applied to them (in the form of trials, stoning, and rejection) shifted them a bit but their relationship with Jesus (and themselves) was able to be restored to equilibrium. In Acts 4, Peter & John spoke before the Sanhedrin - amazing feat for 2 non-descript personalities from the backwater of the Middle East! Clearly, they would never have been able to do this if the foundations of a strong relationship had never been laid. God has placed us in communities of family, work and neighbourhoods to effect change. We will be able to withstand the oncoming stresses ONLY if we allow the Lord to bring us to equilibrium with those we interact with. Like molecules, we must be eager for reactions to take place...to bring about change. And you thought molecules were inanimate objects!

Even though you may be going through change, isn't it a blessing that there are days when no one can see the turmoil underneath?

Update: On subsequent assessments, you won't believe how many students explained Le Chatelier's principle with Giovanni and Danielle!

Count your blessings

1. Are you at equilibrium?

   Yes   **No**   **[Circle one]**

2. If you imagine the spokes of a wheel as various aspects of a typical life – relationships, work, hobbies, marriage, finances – would your relative contentedness in each area make yours a perfect wheel?

   Yes   **No**   **[Circle one]**

3. Which areas of your life could benefit most from being at equilibrium?
   - Spousal relationship
   - Relationship with my children
   - Relationship with my siblings
   - My attitude towards work
   - Financial needs
   - Any other areas?

Blessing 12: If they only knew
Proverbs 22:6

Today I had a very emotional meeting with a student and her mother. Bernice is a beautiful, talented and mature young woman who is feeling displaced and alone. One wonders why.

She was one of the first grade 9 students who caught my eye in the first week of school. Here was a student whom I was going to inspire. Here was a student whom I could groom, to not only be smart but also to appreciate the beauty that God had given her. And as a teacher, this type of student doesn't come along too often. In fact, the last 'mini-me' I had was about ten years ago...my first year of teaching high school. So imagine my pain to discover her slipping away in October, barely into the semester. It started with a missed day here and there, a vacant look, a disinterested shrug.

My skin was beginning to prickle with a negative sort of anticipation, what I call anti-anticipation. Being so busy, I ignored the warning signs. And yet they kept coming. About four weeks ago, she and her new found valley girl friends were giggling as they came into my room, bursting to tell me that a grade twelve boy was interested in her. Oh my, I thought. This is not good. But it would account for a whole lot of changes I'd seen. The vacant stare, the sudden interest in hiking up the school skirt, the extra makeup (nice, mind you but unusual). I prepped myself up to hear what the latest thing was in high school *girlworld!* I asked her to stay in at lunch and tried to have a talk but it didn't go as far as I wanted it to. I was trying to remind her not to leave her smarts behind in pursuit of high school happiness – if such a thing exists. The more we spoke, the more I realized that for most kids, being liked (and ultimately being popular) completely supersedes a whole lot of commonsense. And being smart is definitely not too cool. So I had to do something. I called Mrs. Stark, our Learning Resource Teacher who helps us meander through the dark underworld of student learning.

We arranged a meeting with mom and I looked forward to meeting the parent of this wonderful young woman.
She arrived and the pain in her eyes was so obvious. She'd cried on the way – I knew that for sure. She was losing her girl and she didn't know what was pulling her away. We called Bernice in and asked her what was going on. In between sobs, she said,
"I don't like it here. I have no real friends. I have no opportunity to make wrong choices'.

Wait a minute, did I hear right? No opportunity to make wrong choices? Here we are, a Christian private school trying to create an environment in which young people can realize their full potential. And some students actually think that means we're not allowing them to make mistakes? For crying out loud, there are mistakes everywhere I turn:
* Today, there were 2 students in the office today, for a one-day suspension. Apparently, they were fighting on the bus!

* A grade 12 student was expelled last week for using an illicit drug during lunch.

* A grade 9 student in my class wore stockings that were non-uniform even though she was fully aware it was not allowed. She was promptly asked to remove them.

Oh, we do allow students to make their own choices. Difference is, we quickly let them know that those choices are wrong and should not happen. Then we reprimand them to let them know we expect them to be accountable for their actions. It's a blessing when you know you are trying your best to raise good kids…and its always a blessing to know others can come alongside and help. We should partner with one another to raise good kids – as teachers and as parents.

Does anyone think that's cool anymore?

Prov 22:6 Train a child in the way he should go and when he is old, he will not turn from it.

Count your blessings

1. Do you have any teens at home or interact with them on a daily basis?

   Yes   **No**   **[Circle one]**

2. Do you sometimes wonder why they think the way they do?

   Yes   **No**   **[Circle one]**

3. Do you remember being a teenager?

   Yes   **Don't want to!**   **[Circle one]**

4. Can you recount a moment in your youth when you did something utterly non-sensical? Something you now look back on with a 'how could I have been so stupid?'.

   _____

   _____

   _____

   _____

What a blessing to be all grown up? (Or maybe not!)

Blessing 13: When in Rome
Esther 3: 1- 5

So the Jews are in exile again, in Babylon after a wicked generation has been carried away by Nebuchadnezzar and as usual, there's major oppression going on. But it's been several generations since the first one arrived so they've sort of been absorbed into the Persian system; they have jobs, they've had kids....life is going on.

Mordecai is a devout Jew who doesn't want to become totally Persian. He's living there but he's not going to do everything the Persians do, like bow to Haman. The bible doesn't say why he didn't want to bow to him but I suspect that in Mordecai's mind, it would be like he was bowing to a god...and to him, Haman could never be YHWH. So he refused to bow. And got in trouble for it. As usual, God had other plans and used his refusal to conform to certain practices to bring about some glorious times for God's people in exile.

Mordecai didn't want to conform to a practice he thought was unholy. Sometimes I don't want to conform to some cultural practices I feel are inconsistent with my current location and lifestyle. Reminds me of a time when I got home in my usual daze and was met by Abeyku (my fourteen year old son) who was splitting his ribs laughing. Being quite knackered, I was not amused. Turns out a lady from a Ghanaian church we frequently attend called to inform me that there was a prayer meeting on Saturday morning at 5am.

5 am?
Who is awake at that time on a Saturday morning?
And pray tell, were those people sleeping on needles?

I let out a shriveled laugh – you know, the kind that would cost five cents if laughs were sold. I then proceeded slowly to the kitchen. I didn't think it was worth the thought. And then the early morning rooster called again...just to make sure that I had got the message about the 5am meeting. Which led me to wonder why we immigrate to new countries, intending to become citizens of that country and yet we transport several inconsistent cultural norms into the new situation. That's not to say these cultural norms are all bad; several cultural norms are great and should be protected at all costs.

But, in a country like Ghana, where unemployment is so high (some estimates put it at close to 50%), many people find that waking up to go to church at 5 am (in pleasant weather) is not a big deal. Church on a Saturday is a stress free environment, one where you can let yourself relax in the knowledge that there is a higher power. And when prayers end around 7am, it's just the right time to eat something before starting the household chores. Thus goes a typical day for a typical family, in a typical village in Ghana.

Rewind to my life here in Canada. After a grueling week of an 8 to 4 job that ends up mostly feeling like 6 to 11 (pm, mind you!), my Saturday morning is close to sacred. In between dreams, I often hear my sons saying to one another:

"Shush, mummy doesn't want to be disturbed...she's tired"

My boys know me. They know the recommended daily allowance of 7 hours sleep doesn't cut it with me – I need close to 10. And since there's no way on earth I can get this on a weekday, I try (Oh my, I try so hard!) to snatch it ALL on Saturday morning. Needless to say, I haven't been too successful.

So hearing that I should come to pray, outside my bed, at 5am was a bit much. I decided to tell God why:

Dear God,
I love you, you know that. But, I'm tired. So tired that I think if I come to church at that time, I will surely pass out. And I do think I can pray just as well at home. I do realize that you encourage us to meet together and worship together. But 5 am?
Love, M

I think he understood. Because they haven't called again. But I've got to get around to telling someone that 5 am in Ghana is not 5am in Canada...according to time zones, its 12am...midnight.

Which is why when in Canada, do what Canadians do...be in bed at 12am!

Ahhh...but what a blessing it is, to be called to pray eh?

Count your blessings

1. Has anyone called you to pray recently?

   Yes　　　**No**　　　　　　**[Circle one]**

2. If you've been called, was it 'inconvenient'?

   Yes　　　**No**　　　　　　**[Circle one]**

3. When do you find it most 'convenient' to pray?

   ○ Very early morning...in your bed

   ○ Very early morning...anywhere

   ○ Late at night when the house is quiet...in your bed

   ○ Anywhere

   ○ Nowhere

4. Do you earnestly want to find a time to pray, even if nothing seems convenient right now?

   Yes　　　　　　**No**　　　　**[Circle one]**

You can pray right now you know?

Blessing 14: What child is this?
Luke 10: 38 – 42

So it's getting to Christmas and the signs are everywhere. And I'm stressed...majorly. Hence this dream. Of me offering to carry my younger sister's baby for her for a few months – because she's really tired. Yes, this was a dream alright!

So mysteriously, her 4 - month old baby appears in my tummy and I get ready to carry it for a while – a few months- and then she has to take it back and carry it to term. And then horror of horrors! Barely has the baby taken up residence in my womb when it grows full speed, to term and is demanding to be born. I go into labour and I'm yelling at Grace that this isn't supposed to be happening. I'm not supposed to be going into labour with HER baby!

"Sorry", she says lamely.

"Sorry? Is that all you can say.... and do?" I madly scream.

We head off to the hospital where the doctor tells us that the baby's head is 'crowning' (silly word isn't it? For that kind of process anyway!). I calmly look at the doctor and say:

"I'd like to request a C-section please".

"I'm sorry Mrs. Ashun but it's too late to get a C-section...the baby's head is crowning"

"I know...I heard you the first time!" I shouted.

Oh God, I thought. I can't go through this again. I cannot and will not go through labour!

I look at Grace who is torn. Between laughing at my predicament (Grace and I spend our lives basically torturing one another and taking great joy in it!), and wishing she was actually giving birth to her own baby. I start sobbing so loudly that I can barely contain myself. This can't be happening to me. I was only supposed to do this for a few months to give my sister a break. I wasn't supposed to relive the pain of labour. And then I woke up with a face wet with tears.

And my little boys think mummy is beyond nightmares? This is the mother of all nightmares!

Dr. Phil would say that labour was so traumatic that I don't want to go there again. You got that right! So as I'm driving to work, I'm reminding myself that I've got to know when to help and how to help...and I don't have to carry someone's child for it to be meaningful. In Luke 10, Jesus is longing to spend time with both Mary and Martha but Martha is too busy preparing to feed everyone. Gotta love her but don't you think she could have left well alone and rested for a bit...and listened to Jesus? Martha wanted to help everyone by doing everything. Knowing her, she'd probably have been the type to carry someone's child 'for a bit'.

Thanks for the dream Lord...lesson well learned. What a blessing to know that I have it within me to do something as giving, as carrying someone else's child?

And all this while I slept? No wonder I need more than 7 hours of sleep!

Count your blessings

1. In the Luke 10 story, are you a Martha, Mary or their brother Lazarus (he of the rising from the dead story...if you do nothing usually (i.e. playing dead), then you're a Lazarus!)

   Martha   Mary   Lazarus   [Circle one]

2. If you're a Martha, why do you feel the need to do so much?

   _____

   _____

   _____

   _____

   _____

3. If you're a Mary, do you sometimes feel guilty not doing the seemingly hard work?

   Yes   No   [Circle one]

4. What can you refrain from doing today...so that you can take a break?

_____

_____

_____

Blessing 15: To each her own
Exodus 4: 10 - 17

I almost killed a student today. Unintentionally. As part of the grade eleven chemistry curriculum, all my students have to independently research a topic and present their findings. It's called an STSE and it encourages students to explore a topic in depth (The chemistry behind it, the technology related to it, societal implications as well as environmental) and present their findings in the form of a presentation to the entire class. So far, they've gone very well and the topics have ranged from the obvious like Greenhouse Gases, to the less obvious like drag racing. Each student has 40 minutes to present their study and in-between, the audience is allowed to ask questions.

Sarah was ready to present today. Apart from saying she was nervous around lunchtime, she seemed good to go – she had her laptop, props and a really neat video to show the class. Her topic was hockey. So she starts and she uses the video as the hook. And it's a hook alright (this is Canada after all) so she completely has the students. But then, for a 'hook', it goes on for way too long so about a minute and a half into it, I said:
"Sarah, since this is a hook, a sort of intro, it shouldn't be too long".
"Ok Dr. Ashun, the whole clip is only 2 minutes long" she replied.
I thought cool. It's about to end then.
It did and then she started disintegrating right before our very eyes. She started slurring her words, her

eyes glazed over and she paused for a long time in between words. IT WAS SCARY! Everyone stiffened around me and my mind raced to figure out the best way to stop this sudden 'death by presentation'.

I calmly spoke to her saying: "Umh...Sarah...do you need a moment? Are you ok? She stared for a second or so and nodded and then proceeded to the next slide. Her face started puffing up and getting red as her speech continued to slur and not make sense. She stared at us like she was waiting for us to say something and her whole body looked weak and helpless. I could take it no longer.

"Sarah, I think you should take a break ok?" She didn't argue with that at all. I motioned to two of her friends to take her outside and tried to regain control of the class. Jack was ready with his presentation so I quickly asked him to present to stop the discussions that were inevitable. He was a good speaker and allowed the class to debate certain issues so in no time, Sarah had been pushed to the back burner and their focus was on something else.

Oh my Lord, I thought. What was all that about? I have never seen anyone so nervous and afraid that his or her bodily functions seem to stop working. I have been nervous before but never to this point. As I watched Jack present, I was reminded of how different we all are in God's sight. Some are great at doing things in front of people and for others, it's just not their gift.

As a teacher though, how do I evaluate these students when one of the components we're trying to teach is the ability to confidently present a finding? Is it possible to go through life without ever having to present an idea or concept to a group of people? Is it fair to ask someone to do something that is obviously so traumatic for her?

Moses was chosen by God to deliver a message to Pharoah but he humbly declined the assignment.
"Ho..w do you expect m-e...me to t-alk...t..to Pharoah? I c..can barely str...string two wor...wor...words along!" (my paraphrase).
Even though he wasn't a great speaker, the Lord knew he could be a great leader and equipped him with a right hand man (Aaron) to help him with the speaking part. Moses must have wondered why God chose him to lead his people when speaking authoritatively was obviously a large part of the job description.

As usual, I don't have the answers...so I've rescheduled Sarah for next week. And I'm praying that my classroom will not be the scene of an incident that appears on the 6 o'clock news. Rather, I'm praying for wisdom to know how to incorporate different types of giftedness into my curriculum.

What a blessing to have different kinds of giftedness?

Update: Sarah did very well her second time around...what a blessing!

Count your blessings.

1. Which of the following can you tick off confidently as a gift you have? (If you're not sure, ask someone!)

    ○ Ability to speak in front of an audience

    ○ Musically gifted

    ○ Academically gifted

    ○ Good with people (i.e. interpersonal skills)

    ○ Detail oriented

    ○ Great attitude

    ○ Kinesthetic (Sporty?)

    ○ Creative (writing, performing, drawing etc)

    ○ Organizer

    ○ _____

2. In what way have you used your gift as a blessing in the past week?

    _____

    _____

Blessing 16: Losing my Marbles
Galatians 5:22

Chemistry started off with Masood giving me a Valentine hug. Masood is a seventeen-year-old Egyptian boy dating a 16-year-old Egyptian girl his parents know nothing about. According to him, he'll be hanged if they find out...ooops, I guess they just did! Masood and Mahdi, his Syrian friend, sit at the front and are either whining about how much work they have to do or about how they can't wait to get married to real Arab girls because they are so 'fit'. Turns out 'fit' is the new 'cool' ...who knew?

Kiko, my 'diminutive' 6 footer of a Korean girl gave me a heart shaped container with chocolates in it. The neat thing is, she actually made them herself! Go figure. Another neat thing is, since she has access to all those things that Asians use to keep healthy like green tea – real green tea – she put them in the chocolates! Look out Laura Secord and Yves Rocher...like all things commercial, the Asians are coming!

We did a boring session (yah, even I thought it was boring) on carboxylic acids and esters – wait a minute, esters are interesting – you get to design banana-flavored stuff and such...it was interesting actually. It got annoying when the usual suspects started complaining about how tough their lives were. Oh yah, they forgot to mention that when they get home from school, mummy has cooked and they just have to eat, get on

MSN, and chat with some other kids who have nothing to do, watch TV, listen to tunes on their ipods and whine again! And all this whining because two teachers happen to have put two quizzes on the same day? Whatever happened to students just toughing it out and realizing that the world is not necessarily a fun place huh? Sometimes, I just want to hold their heads, shake them a bit and scream into their ears "Grow up"! And now I sound bitter but I'm not...seriously...I'm just really worried about the state of our students and what kind of future awaits them if someone doesn't make them sit up and realize that the world isn't waiting to spoon feed them. Ugh!

So, I finish whining myself, class is over and I walk out to the office. Of course there's a pile of mail in my box and some kids have pretended to put stuff in and faked the date so its not late...what do they think I am....stupid?

The office is somber because of the death of a school parent who was very active in the school. I quietly take my pile of assignments and walk out into a sea of students just milling around in valentine clothing...apparently it's Valentines day! The girly girls are all in pink and those boys brave enough not to be labeled 'other' are in pink shirts...where do they pick that up from? Salvation Army thrift store? Anyway, Jamaican patties are on sale and I go and 'take' one and congratulate Nadia and the girls on a superb job done today at assembly. My second class is about to walk in...the grade 11's are quite a challenge. I have 26 of them and I can almost bet my....my....my husband...that only 5 want to be in that class!! According to the Education Act (or some other nondescript piece of legislation), they have to have one senior science credit and they all think taking Workplace Science is like being a loser. Science is not for everyone and you may be a science loser but a music genius. Anyway, today was a quiz so in 'spoilt child world', there was major panic with comments like:

"I didn't even know we had a quiz".
"When did we study this?"
"Is it in the book?"
You bet my... (Lord help me find a good word here!). It's in the book, I wanted to shout but of course that would not be professional or ladylike and I'd like to think I can be both...on a good day! I reminded myself that I was there to 'influence and challenge young minds' (this last line said with a James Earl Jones kind of voice).

Well, I once taught a grade 10 science class that was filled with misfits...students who'd taken the course 10 times (or so it seemed), those who needed the credit to be able to graduate but couldn't get into an advanced course and those who would have been in special Ed but were 'trying' to get a 'real' course. It was pathetic. One girl would take phone calls during class apparently for her mom...they had an escort service and she manned the phones. A group of 'high' students were constantly playing cards at the back of the class and when I asked them for it, they hid them on themselves and I couldn't seize them. Another two just talked about guns all period and sat at the front of the class – like they wanted to learn how to mix chemicals to put into guns or bombs for that matter.

I asked my mentor how she survived and like a true veteran, she said she survived because she had to. Some of those kids just had to get the credit and leave – they weren't destined for university and they knew it. This was obvious one afternoon when we had hardly anyone show up for the class and walked out to the lobby to see what was going on. There was a mini career fair for the armed forces and police and that's where most of our students were. I heard Adam asking the recruiter
"And we really get to hold guns? Real guns?" I felt the battle for their minds was lost at that point!

Teachers at this school seemed upbeat despite some of the frustrating situations. I couldn't see how I could ever teach in a school like that until I met an old friend, someone I had taught with in a previous school sitting & having lunch in the teachers lounge area. I made a beeline for him and asked him what he was doing there, 'did he teach here'? Turns out he was supply teaching and when he said he loved it there, I thought he was missing a few marbles.

"Stop playing me" I said, to which he shook his head letting me know he wasn't playing me. What the heck was he talking about? How could he love it here? Turns out, he supply teaches all over the place and actually thinks this place is normal. Normal? I scream silently...how can this be normal and is this what I'm going to have for the rest of my NORMAL life? I'm struggling to find the blessing here....

Paul encouraged the Galatians to pray for the fruits of the spirit so the spirit would lead them. These fruits were love, joy, peace, patience, kindness, goodness, faithfulness, gentleness and self-control. Phew! Oh Lord, I need your joy, which can only come when I ask you to dwell within me. I need the fruits of the spirit especially patience...every second, every minute and every hour of every day. Amen.

Update: I found the blessing!!! When things seem so 'impassable' (like the Red Sea for the Israelites), it is possible that God can show us a way: several students tell me I've been their 'way...Ironically, some have been my way too!

Count your blessings

1. Do you sometimes wonder if you should leave your current place of work?

   Yes   **No**   **[Circle one]**

2. Why do you want to leave?

   _____
   _____

3. What could change your mind?

   - ○ Change of environment, same job
   - ○ Change of job, same environment
   - ○ Change of job, change of environment
   - ○ Just quit life!

4. Can you think of one thing you'll miss if you leave?

   _____

5. Could this one thing make you more content at work?

   Yes   **No**   **[Circle one]**

Consider it a blessing to have a place to go on Monday morning…and you get paid too!

Blessing 17: The 8:05 from Union Station
Genesis 16

J oe is out at his company Christmas party so I'm home with the kids. Although I'm glad I didn't go because I feel tired, I'm wondering what's going on there. So the jealousy bug is biting and there's no reason why I should feel jealous. Oh wait a minute...at last week's company dinner (his company seems to have them every week!), this lady was trying to tell him something and pulled his head closer...I was not amused. Naaa...just kidding.

I realize I have a choice. To stew in jealousy, mistrust and worry or to love, cherish, and to trust. I'd rather choose the latter set of actions. But when I hear that marriages around me are disintegrating, (and some are very close) I wonder how 'love' can suddenly 'go away'. Whatever happens to the "I will never leave you", "I'll love you forever", and "You're my life" slogans that are part and parcel of a new relationship? It scares me to think that what once looked hopeful can suddenly look so hopeless. And the pain that goes along with that...it's hard to miss it in the voice of anyone going through a separation or divorce.

Dad and I visited a wonderful couple last weekend who had just celebrated their 50th wedding anniversary a couple of months ago. Now bear in mind that I'd just met these people and yet I was still able to see the hallmarks of a great relationship:

- Respect for one another
- Respect for each other's giftings and capabilities
- The excitement at doing things together and having shared interests.
- A common set of values

This was obvious the moment we walked through the door and the husband said:

"Jessie has told me so much about you".

Ah hah I thought. They talk to each other! They share their experiences everyday. Even the mundane ones. So they seem to have it down pat...but that's not to say that everything in their relationship is perfect...we know it can't be.

I'm quite sure that there is no magic formula that gets you the perfect spouse or relationship. Like most things in life, it takes careful thought and planning, has to mature over a long period of time, and takes an awful lot of patience!

Abraham and Sarah had an imperfect relationship. In that culture, 'bearing children' was a sure sign that the Lord had blessed you. Without children, Sarah must have felt unhappy, alone, unloved and definitely unblessed. The bible tells us Sarah was the one who suggested that Abraham have an affair with Hagar, her Egyptian maidservant. Quite weird that a wife would suggest that but it was another time and another culture so who are we to judge? I can imagine the stresses that were wrought in the family when Ishmael - the son of the affair - was born.

Sarah: Does he still love me?
Abraham: Now she's having my baby, do I still see her? How can I do that and still make time to let Sarah know I care?
Hagar: I got her man!

Like a train patiently traveling a well-worn track, at 15 years of marriage, Joe and I are still on track. Every station we pull into has its own issues. But we stay on the train, enjoying the view, sharing our thoughts and wondering why some of the people who were on the train with us, have gotten off. We miss them. And how confusing when we see them at other stations...with different people?

They look happier though.

I pray that the Lord will bless our relationships wherever we might be. That he'll open our eyes to see the beauty in one another...and in so doing, give us the patience and trust that will help to keep us on track. God wants us to be content in his love. Look around you...do you see God's love?

That's a blessing for sure!

Count your blessings

1. Are you married?

   Yes   **No**   **[Circle one]**

2. If you answered No to #1, is it because you 'got off the train'?

   Yes   **No**   **n/a**   **[Circle one]**

3. If you're still 'on the train', how can you make the experience more enjoyable? (See the following suggestions in the light of being on a train)

   o Pull the blinds and let more light in?

   o Bring a pillow on board so your backs are more comfortable?

   o Letting her (or him) sit at the window seat...even if you want the window seat.

   o Bring some board games (or cards) because it can be quite a long journey!

Blessing 18: Ut Omnes Unum Sint
(That all may be one)
Romans 3: 9 - 12

I heard an insightful speaker this morning at R & D. Professor Bowen from Redeemer University gave us insight into how our students perform when they enter university; specifically how graduates of Christian high schools perceive their role as students compared to graduates of secular public schools. She shared how our graduates seemed to have knowledge of the order of creation, scriptural narrative and lots of doctrine. They have a moral code and they tend to be service oriented. However, they seem to have lost excitement about their faith and have no desire to go beyond their comfort zone and explore other worldviews. Many were basically quite intolerant of others who didn't believe what they believed.

That got me wondering about something I heard this morning on the radio. Andy Barrie, one of my favorite talk show personalities was talking about a judge in Toronto who had a Christmas tree, originally in the foyer of the courthouse moved to the back – because it was oppressive to non-Christians. The audience was asked to call in and share their opinions on the subject and call in line was jammed!

First caller went something like this:
"Umh...as I child, I felt excluded from Christmas because my family was not Christian and I agree with the judge. We shouldn't have to have someone else's religion forced

on us. If people want to see a tree, they should get one themselves"

"I'm with you" Andy said. "I'm also not a Christian".

Bam! My world developed a disappointing hole at that point. I'd like to say I didn't know why I was disappointed but that's not the truth. I know that many people aren't Christians. But maybe, because I enjoyed his commentaries, views and opinions, I thought he and I would be more alike...and it hurt that he didn't believe what I believed, even though he doesn't even know me.

Second caller:
"Get over it! Why do we make such a big deal every year about this? We live in a multicultural country and have to learn to celebrate with others even when we don't share their faith. Why do we need to change the name from a 'Christmas Tree' to a 'Holiday Tree'? Why is it ok to call the symbol of Hannukah the Menorah, when we can call it the Holiday Candle Set? Enough already! We talk of including everyone in this wonderful mosaic we call Canada and yet when Christmas comes up, we debate the tree – which is never even mentioned in the bible!"
Needless to say, I agreed with him. And sort of liked him. And I don't even know him.

Which led me to wonder...am I a bigot? Do I like people who only believe what I believe? I don't think so! I know lots of Christians I don't like much. They have opinions that are not mine. And I also know some non-Christians who hold some of my opinions...and I enjoy interacting with them. In Romans 3, Paul declares that there is none righteous...that Jews and Gentiles alike are all under sin. How mortifying for those who think being a Christian makes them 'better' than someone else?

When I was six, my family moved to England and one of the families we interacted with regularly were the Khans. Dr. Khan was a Bangladeshi Muslim and along with his wife Shahana, his children Bolaka, Shajeeb and Shalme, they showed us that not all Muslims belonged to the Al Fateh movement or had studied military tactics with Hezbollah. They would visit us at Christmas and we would visit them at Eid. Through that simple gesture, we opened our minds to another worldview not too different from our own. And without using pat phrases like "Give a Mennonite a hug today" or "Honk if you're Ukrainian orthodox", we can, in our own ways embrace different worldviews and yet rest assured of our own faith.

Yes, it is possible...and when I went into my grade 9 class this morning, it was confirmed. After showing a DVD about Space (from The Discovery Channel), the class erupted in a discussion about the age of the earth and other celestial bodies. After hearing the different views – which ranged from old earth to new earth – it was comforting to tell the students that whatever they believed, there was one unified concept.

We all felt blessed to be living on a wonderfully created Earth!

Count your blessings

1. Do you have friends who don't have the same religious beliefs as you do?

   Yes   **No**   **[Circle one]**

2. What are some of these religions?

   _____

3. What would you do if while standing in line to get on a plane at the airport, you turned around and noticed a man wearing a turban about three spots behind you...also waiting to get on board?

   _____

   _____

   _____

   _____

These questions should challenge our worldviews...and remind us that it is a blessing to have different people in our world!

Blessing 19: Rush Hour 3
Matthew 6: 25 – 34

To: *anyone@stressed.com*
Hey there,
Tuesday passed in a blur - school/work, meeting till 5 after school, rushed home, dropped Abeyku at football practice, rushed home to monitor Kwam and Jojo's homework, bathe them, put them to bed, go back and pick Abeyku up, come home, help him with homework, do my prep for school tomorrow, go upstairs (pass family room on the way and observe with nonchalance, the steady buildup of disorder...do I care?), lie in bed and flip channels hoping something is boring enough to lull me off to sleep but there are too many to choose from, read Imperium, drop Imperium by bedside, try to turn bedside lamp off without knocking it down, go to sleep.....in dreamland.....is that the beginning of a cough I hear? Look at the clock, its only 5am and Kwam is hacking...annoying allergies...so I'm up...writing to you!
I seriously need a break...

Have you felt like this before? Like a hamster on its wheel, going nowhere? Doing the same things over and over again....and still going nowhere? In Matthew 6, the Lord reminds us not to worry about what we will eat, drink and wear...because he's going to provide. Isn't it comforting to read in the latter part of verse 26 " ...are you not much more valuable than they?"

Have we ever felt blessed to be stressed? Sounds like an oxymoron but my stresses exist because I have people in my life – whether at home or work. And isn't that a blessing?

Count your blessings

1. There are families and then there are *families* – you know, those that are so close they could really be like family. Who's in your *family*?

    _____

    _____

    _____

2. Be honest...how many of them stress you out?

    Just one   3 or more   All of them!   [Circle one]

3. Can you write a prayer for this person (or these people)?

    _____

    _____

4. How about writing a prayer for yourself...that you will start seeing these stresses as opportunities to be a blessing to others?

    _____

    _____

    _____

Blessing 20: ABBA relived
1 Samuel 2: 12 – 26

Growing up is never easy I know
But I have to go
Knowing me knowing you, it's the best I can do

ABBA's ringing in my ears as I wonder how to explain for the nth time to my 14 year old why he can't go to a new years eve party with his best friend.

"But mom, it's New Years Eve. Everyone goes to parties."

"But we'd like to be in church on New Years Eve…sort of ushering in the New Year in the house of God".

"Oh mum…does every New Year's Eve have to be spent 'ushering in the New Year in the house of God?" (this latter said in a mocking tone). And I'm definitely not amused.

This particular friend is not all bad…he's just sort of bad. In a curly haired, cutesy sort of way – like Hugh Grant. But he's one year older than Abeyku, more world-wise, crude and not really into the niceties of life. For example, when he comes to visit, he never greets us. Big deal you say? Yep, I do think it's a big deal. Because my son knows that entering someone's house is a privilege and on entering, if the parents are in, you say:

"Hi Mr. (or Mrs.) Somebody". So this guy sort of gives me mini-creeps. Just a little bit. Because I trust my boy. He is the kind of child who greets adults respectfully, comes home when he's supposed to (most of the time!), does what is right (mostly!) and is genuinely a good boy. But he's 14 going on 30 so he thinks he should be able to do things he feels like even if his battle weary parents think he's not ready. What to do?

He's angry with me for telling him he's not old enough to go to a party with a family we don't interact with and who don't seem to have the same values as we do. I'm sitting in bed and he's trudging off crying...not understanding.

Gotta be tough and stand my ground. Knowing what I know, an all night party is not a good idea. As I ponder all these things in my heart, Kwam (our 8 yr old) walks in and asks why Abeyku is upset.
"What's wrong with him mum?"
"He wants to go to a party with James and I said no".
"Why can't he go to the party?"
"It ends at 2 am".
"Oh..." he mumbles knowingly.
"And he's also only 14".
"That's really old mum"
"I know Kwam....he's way older than you" And also quite responsible. So why do I feel in my spirit that it's not a good idea? He knows not to ask his dad. Thinking he'd get an easier ride, he came to me. No cigar.

Eli's sons were so bad; they never listened to their dad when he warned them about sinning against the Lord. I can imagine that he'd been very lenient with them in their youth. Or maybe not. I don't know. But the story of Eli and his sons teaches me that when the spirit of the Lord prompts me about decisions we make as a parent team, I know I have to listen...even when my child thinks I'm the meanest thing that walked the earth.

I pray for you Abeyku (and Kwam and Jojo) that you will "grow in stature and in favor with both God and man". I have no doubt that one-day, you'll understand... and feel blessed that I was your mom...

Count your blessings

1. Do you have a teen at home?

Yes   **No**

Not sure, haven't seen them in a while!

2. How many times have you heard the scream "That's not fair?

   Once   **twice**

Too many times!   [Circle one]

3. Do you sometimes feel yourself buckling under the pressure to give in?

   Yes   **No**   **[Circle one]**

4. What are some of the measures you've taken that have <u>NOT</u> worked?

_____

_____

5. Which measures have worked?

_____

_____

Keep doing them! Remember that you DO know a whole lot more than they do!!

Blessing 21: Payback
2Timothy 1:1-7

I haven't been this mad at my mother since becoming an adult. I thought that as an adult, I'd now understand everything she does and why she does it but this latest incident has just blown my mind away.

For the past week, she has been steadily declining in health and it got so bad three days ago that she drove herself to the emergency room asking to see her doctor because her shoulder felt inexorably sore. She couldn't be seen but she was booked for later on in the week and sent home. She was so sore that dad had to do the cooking...and it's a mercy that the house didn't burn down. Now for someone who so loves doing everything for everyone, for her to not lift a finger shows how awful she was feeling.

So Joe and I are enjoying some alone time at the kitchen table with the kids all in bed and who comes traipsing up the stairs? Mother! In her work clothes! With her neck throbbing visibly and a guilty look on her face!
"Where are you going?" I asked truculently.
"Work", she replied truculently also.

Mum works as a personal support worker in an elderly care facility and she loves it. She always wanted to be a nurse but grew up with no dad and a farmer for a mom. Her schooling was sporadic to say the least and at a time when Ghana was experiencing a shortage of teachers, students who had barely finished high school were allowed to go for teacher training. Which she did, so she ended up as an elementary school teacher. A job she didn't love and which she gladly gave up for being a stay at home mom when kids came along. Fast forward to age 60, and she's graduating from the PCP diploma program from a local community college in Ontario and boy were we all so proud of her!

"Why are you going to work when you're not well yourself?" I continued.

"They have no one else to take my shift".

"But you could have called them to request a shift change" I argued.

This back and forth continued but she still left the house...and left me wondering why she would still want to go to work looking so sick. And it was her birthday too! Did she feel the need to feel needed? Is she now doing what she feels she should have done her whole life and so she thinks illness shouldn't take her away from it? Why do I feel like the parent?

I feel guilty because I can remember being young and brainless and doing stuff that made my mom mad...and sad. I seemed to care less how much she thought of me and felt like she didn't understand what I needed to do. Somehow, I think there's been a role reversal. Mom doesn't want to give up something that means a lot to her...and I don't want to lose someone I love. But we don't understand each other at this point. I want her to stay home and rest and she wants to be out, being active, helping others and ultimately fulfilling a dream.

It is a blessing that mom is still alive and mostly well and wanting to help others. It's a blessing that she has goals she wants to fulfill in the time she has left. And it sure is a blessing that I'm alive to see a mom who does what's good for others.

Timothy's mother Eunice and grandmother Lois exhibited characteristics that Paul said he saw in Timothy: sincere faith I quite remember. Am I like my mom? Can I be that giving? Am I
that stubborn or will I become that stubborn as I grow older? How much of her is in me and can I stop her stubbornness from becoming mine when I'm her age? How can I show concern and yet still be supportive of what she wants to do with her life?

Oh mum!

Count your blessings

1. Do any of your parents live close by?

Yes   **No**   **[Circle one]**

2. Do you feel that they need you so much more now than before?

Yes   **No**   **[Circle one]**

3. What situation has highlighted this need?

_____
_____
_____

4. Do you feel yourself pulled in two directions – one way by your children and the other by your aging parents – knowing that both need you?

Yes   **No**   **[Circle one]**

5. What are you doing to stop yourself being resentful and focusing instead on making the years they have left meaningful ...for both of you?

_____
_____
_____
_____

Cherish the times you spend with your mom or dad...they won't be around forever!

Blessing 22: O come let us adore!

Christmas is over but the Ashun household has something beautiful to celebrate this morning. Amaris, my sister Grace's baby was born at 10:25 last night and what a joy to behold the whole spectacle! From the time of the first contractions to the joyous 'beholding'...what an amazing gift God gives us when he blesses us with a pure human specimen?

After hearing from school that it was a snow day, I immediately got into my car to start the arduous drive to my sister Grace's house. Snow hardly shuts anything down in Ontario so for this to warrant it, it meant that the trip to my younger sister's house - which normally takes half an hour - was going to drag on for the worst part of two hours. Still, I had to go. How could I give up the pleasure of seeing Grace contort in pain? She and I go on at each other in a 'loving' way but I just could not wait to see her face when she realized that labour pains are what they are...a lot of labour and major pint of pain!

I became my usual 'loving' self and massaged her back while the contractions came and went and then had to leave to pick my children up from school. I didn't hear from her again till six in the evening, by which time she was in hospital with Johnson and mum...who were both majorly stressing out! Turns out Amaris had done a twister in the tummy and wound the cord around her neck 5 times! What is this child thinking? Even Saddam had it once round *his* neck for crying out loud!!

Insensitive, I know, but you get the picture? This was frightening!

A night nurse was the one who told us she had been wheeled to the Operating Room for a C-section and then mum stepped up the ante...she should surely be in movies because she really knows how to make you afraid when you're trying not to be. Her eyeballs popping out in fear, her fists clenched, she started blabbering about how scared she was.

"Hold yourself together mummy" I said..."its only surgery"

What a silly comment to make to a woman with five children of her own – three born in deepest darkest Africa without the benefit of the mod cons! She started remembering all those who'd died in childbirth....ahhhh...I had to shut her up by telling dad to talk to her! So here I am, the presumed fortress of calm, beginning to buckle under the stress & pressure. I go to the washroom to do some breathing exercises and tell myself that I am going to be strong. I walk out and Johnson comes to us with the biggest smile ever...

"It's a girl!" Mummy fainted. Or so it seemed.

I, on the other hand was very much alive, jumping for joy, hugging Johnson and completely ignoring mother who had collapsed on the floor in relief...crying, laughing...all at the same time.
"I knew it, she said, I knew it".
I refrained from asking her what she knew...mum was not in a state to remember anything she knew!

We went in to see mother and child and I fell in love. Here was a girl who had beautiful hair, long legs and eyes that refused to close. And what was that? It looked like a mouth that would be talking back...soon.

Close to perfection... and the Lord has blessed us all with her.

For unto us, Amaris is born...

Email: drmaryashun@rogers.com